GETTING A SQUIRREL TO FOCUS
IN THE VIRTUAL WORLD
NOT JUST CONTENT, BUT CONNECTION

GETTING A SQUIRREL TO FOCUS
IN THE VIRTUAL WORLD

NOT JUST CONTENT, BUT CONNECTION

©2020 by Uhmms Publishing

Media, Pennsylvania 19063

Uhmms offers excellent discounts on this book when ordered in quantity for bulk purchase or special sales. For more information, please contact Uhmms Publishing.

www.uhmms.com
improve@uhmms.com

Printed in the United States of America

First printing: December 2020

ISBN-13: 978-0-9861248-1-5

As the world continues to change around us, we gain a deeper appreciation for things that can and do remain constant in life. As the African proverb reminds us, "When the root is deep, there is no reason to fear the wind." I have been incredibly fortunate to have been given solid roots from my mother, who provided the example of a strong work ethic and unrelenting determination. The roots were strengthened again through the love and support of my amazing daughter, Emily, and wonderful husband, Dan, who have never once wavered in their commitment to my personal and professional success. Because of their confidence, I do not fear the wind and have branched out in many directions that would have been impossible on my own. I am overwhelmed with gratitude.

Table of Contents

About the Author

Dr. Patricia Scott will help you speak, lead, and inspire and can enhance any presentation, conversation, negotiation, sales call, or interview. Her specialty is teaching the tools and strategy to break through distraction. In today's world with so much noise, she can help you get your message heard.

Dr. Scott is an established expert and leader in the field of communication and has the experience and credentials to offer her clients a unique blend of time-tested strategies and real-world application:

- More than 15 years of corporate leadership experience

- National best-selling author of *Getting a Squirrel to Focus: Engage and Persuade Today's Listeners* and *Getting a Squirrel to Focus: Don't Just Inform, Transform Your Audience.*

- One of Inc. Magazine's Top 100 Leadership Speakers of 2018

- Master of Ceremonies for an event focusing on world peace at the United Nations in New York

- Panelist on "Women Empowerment, the 2030 agenda for UNSDG" sponsored by King Hamad Global Centre for Peaceful Coexistence - with her excellency Sumaya Meer from Bahrain.

- Featured interview on Forbes.com
- Featured instructor for Udemy and LeadX
- B.A., M.A., and Ph.D. in Communication
- Lecturer in the Communication Program at the Wharton School, University of Pennsylvania, since 2004, as well as lecturing for the Wharton MBA for Executives Program and the Wharton Executive Education Program at the Aresty Institute for Executive Education
- Member of advisory board for the Master of Arts program in Corporate Communication for Baruch College of the City University of New York since 2008
- Four-time invited speaker at the Conference on Corporate Communication (in association with Corporate Communication International at Baruch College, City University of New York) in Wroxton, England, New York, and Hong Kong
- Awarded "Best Paper of Conference" for analysis of social, task, and semantic networks of knowledge workers, at her first academic conference
- Published in *Corporate Communications: An International Journal,* a peer-reviewed scholarly journal (Emerald Publications)

Dr. Scott specializes in the art and science of communication and will help you polish your skills, build your confidence and make your personal communication more effective. Whether it is public speaking, persuasion, data presentation, facilitation, or skillful conversations, her methods can enhance any communication. These strategies have proven effective across many industries such as technology, pharmaceuticals and medical device companies.

Through keynote addresses, workshops, and e-learning, she provides a communication strategy so that your message can be heard loud and clear, despite all the noise around us. Satisfied clients include ADP, Advanced Bionics, AO North America, AO Spine, AstraZeneca, Bank of America, Bristol Meyers-Squibb, Brunswick Group, Chemtura, Drexel University, EMD Serono, Emergent Biosolutions, Endo Pharmaceuticals, Fresenius Medical Care, Genentech, Gilead, Johnson and Johnson, Knowles Electronics, Medartis, Medtronic, Merck, Otsuka, Pilling-Weck, Purdue Pharma, Regeneron, Sandoz, Sanofi–Genzyme, Shire, Storeroom Solutions, Stryker, Synthes, Takeda, Temple University, Unisys, Valeant, Valtronic, Vericel, Vertebron and West Pharmaceutical.

Introduction

Are your virtual sales engagements, meetings, training workshops, going better than they were at first but still not good enough? Are you not sure whether you're accomplishing your objectives for the virtual interaction? Do you have difficulty transitioning from a discussion about how everyone is doing to business? Are you confident that you're engaging the meeting participants?

If the quality of your virtual interactions is not quite where to want it to be, perhaps that is because we need virtual engagement tactics and strategy.

Just because virtual communication is the new norm doesn't mean we have evolved.

COVID-19 changed the world in many ways. Most tragically, of course, in just the first 8 months after the disease was declared a pandemic by the World Health Organization in March of 2020, over 1.3 million people died across the globe. In addition, the social and economic disruption that COVID-19 caused sparked the largest global recession since the Great Depression. Businesses who were still able to operate, had to redefine how they interacted with their employees and customers.

Hundreds if not thousands of articles, webinars, e-learnings and job aids offer you help to run a successful virtual meeting or presentation. And yet, I often get called for more help. Why?

We've learned that the camera has to be near eye level, so people don't feel as if they are looking up our noses. We know that what's in the background can be distracting, because we'd rather take a visual tour of an interesting office than listen to the message. We make sure everyone starts the meeting on mute. We've even figured out that if you are in front of a window or bright light, you'll look like you're in some kind of witness protection program.

We can do what's mandatory to make the meeting run smoothly. Some more advanced facilitators have figured out how to make it (sometimes awkwardly) more interactive. Yet we would rarely rate a virtual meeting as good or successful.

In the rush to create a "smooth" meeting, the strategy of engaging our audiences has gone by the wayside. The computer or phone screen is creating a barrier, a challenge to be overcome.

I have spent the past decade or so writing books and giving keynotes and workshops about how today's audiences have evolved. I have emphasized the need for relevance and what we have learned from the study of communication and neuroscience that can help us provide value instead of just more information.

My two books, "Getting a Squirrel to Focus: Engage and Persuade Today's Listener" and "Getting a Squirrel to Focus on Presentations: Don't Just Inform, Transform Your Audience," revolve around the metaphor of giving a nut to a squirrel during a conversation or slide presentation. As you probably have noticed, squirrels have relatively short attention spans and behave in a jumpy, sporadic, and distracted manner, much like today's listeners. But when that squirrel eats a nut, he sits still, he's focused, and his attention span increases by 23,900%. I have created the ACORN Communication Strategy™ for conversations and the WALNUT Presentation Strategy™ for slide presentations. Both strategies are buckets of tools that enhance your ability to get your message out and engage with your audience.

The strategy you will learn in this book will enhance your ability to communicate virtually.

Our communication environment has been changing for decades, and our listeners are different than they were even 10 years ago. We have more distractions and more competing sources of information than ever.

The same communication skills that have made you successful in your career are unlikely to be the same communication skills that will keep you successful.

Our audiences are evolving away from us at an alarming rate, and if we do not evolve our communication skills and strategies to keep up, we will become extinct communicationally. Through the study of neuroscience and communication, we have identified two fundamental shifts in the way we take information in.

The first shift is in the value of information. In the past, information was scarce, so it had a lot more value than it does today. We will never have to know or memorize anything ever again; we just have to be curious enough to look it up. What is scarce now is meaning and connection.

Your role can no longer be simply to provide information; you have to be a meaning finder and provide insight and value.

You have to connect the dots between the information and the value the listener will gain from it. We don't just want information, we want meaning. We don't want just want facts, we want insight. Providing the value of relevance and insight is even more difficult in virtual interactions. Why should someone engage with you in a virtual meeting if they can find the answer quicker with a Google search?

The second shift is in attention span. People are more distracted now than they have ever been. With the flood of information, we search quickly for what we want and ignore what we don't want. Since we have so much more information and so many more choices, we can be more selfish in the hunt for relevance. We get what we want when we want it, and when we want it is right now.

Now, communicators have to not only deal with an audience that has a short attention span, we have to try to engage virtually rather than face to face. During virtual meetings, in addition to the normal distractions, we have been thrust into an unfamiliar landscape with a host of new distractions.

This meme created by Sarah Woodard went viral when she posted it on Facebook. She found it felt weird to watch herself talking and working and chronicled how she felt distracted during a Zoom meeting early in the COVID-19 pandemic.

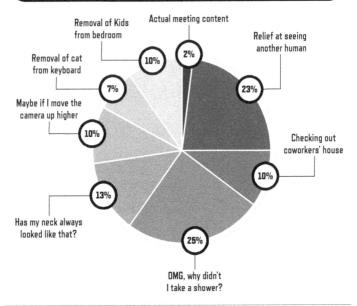

Virtual Meeting Attention Span

Removal of Kids from bedroom — 10%

Actual meeting content — 2%

Relief at seeing another human — 23%

Removal of cat from keyboard — 7%

Maybe if I move the camera up higher — 10%

Checking out coworkers' house — 10%

Has my neck always looked like that? — 13%

OMG, why didn't I take a shower? — 25%

Sarah Woodard[1]

Conducting ourselves in the virtual world is tougher on everyone. The presenter, like the audience, has trouble maintaining focus and having the energy to engage the audience. Do you feel exhausted at the end of a long virtual day? It is not just your imagination, and you are not alone. In a survey of 1,620 participants from 90 countries, 84% of respondents found virtual communication to be more difficult than in-person communication.[2] Even if you have a technically smooth virtual session, it is just not the same as face-to-face communication. Five main factors make virtual communication more difficult for us.

First, according to Gianpiero Petriglieri, a researcher on sustainable learning and development in the workplace and an associate professor at the INSEAD Graduate School of Business, we need to work harder when we communicate virtually. When we are virtual, it is harder for us to see and process nonverbal cues like body language and facial expressions. It is also harder to process and assign meaning to tone and pitch of voice.[3]

Second, even something as natural as silence may be viewed skeptically. A study from 2014 showed that on the telephone, a speaker who paused for as little as 1.2 seconds "was rated to be less friendly, less active, less cheerful, less self-efficient, less achievement-striving, and less self-disciplined."[4]

The third factor is eye contact. In humans, eye contact helps us communicate intention and regulate our interactions. From a young age, we prefer looking at eyes more than at any other facial feature. An entire academic discipline is devoted to gaze processing and its biological significance. Studies show that people prefer a long gaze to frequent very short ones, and we interpret a somewhat longer gaze as a sign that a person likes us more. Conversely, overly long or overly short gazes can be discomfiting.

UK researchers measured, across a wide range of ages, cultures, and personality types, what duration of eye contact was considered "normal" and what duration of eye contact makes us feel uncomfortable. The participants in the study had a preferred gaze duration of 3.3 seconds.[5]

While we obviously look at each other and make eye contact when we are face-to-face, we don't intentionally stare at each other. The constant and unyielding gaze that we feel through the camera makes us fatigued. Imagine walking into a conference room and having 15 of your colleagues all stare at you at the same time. Now imagine they've all moved within 12 inches of your face. That would be enough to exhaust anyone!

This is a good reason, when you're designing your strategy, to include interactive elements that can shorten a long span of having participants looking at each other.

The fourth consideration is that we don't usually watch ourselves work and speak, so looking at ourselves on camera makes us overly conscious of how we behave. We work harder and feel more stress because we are very aware of being watched and feel an increasing need to "perform" and meet social norms. It's hard enough to "read" a room when we are physically in it. The problem is compounded when we have to read many (virtual) rooms at the same time and try to fit in.[6]

And finally, we are also aware that the line between work and home has become blurred. Most of us now not only work from the same place that we live, we also work on the same platforms that we use to socialize. Happy hours and visits with family and friends happen the same way we do work. And when we are working, we have to manage our families by asking them to be quiet and hide. For many of us, our work/life balance has become almost impossible to manage, as events overlap.

A study titled "Self-Complexity and Affective Extremity: Don't Put All of Your Eggs in One Cognitive Basket" showed that if we are able to maintain greater distinction between the various aspects of self (worker, spouse, friend, parent, mentor, etc.), we are more likely to maintain positive feelings about some aspects and buffer against negative feelings. For example, we may feel good about the parent we are; then, if work is not going well, we can compartmentalize those feelings and keep them separate. But if every aspect of our self begins to overlap, self-complexity theory has shown that we may be more prone to depression.[7]

All these factors make it hard for us to relax into a virtual conversation or present in a natural way to deliver a concise message that is meaningful to our audience. Our idea of a normal audience experience has also changed yet again. So how can we make virtual meetings and presentations better for us and our audience? It is not as easy as taking content that would have been delivered face-to-face and offering it the same way virtually. Trying to get the attention of the listener has always been important, but now, more than ever, what we crave is connection. We have to continue to be allowed to be human even when we are mediated by our communication channel.

I created the ALMOND Virtual Communication Strategy™ to help us think through the strategy of how virtual engagement can get better for everyone. Some of the tools listed below are borrowed from my other two communication strategies for conversations and slide presentations because, no matter the method, live or virtual, there are universal truths that apply to engaging today's listeners. Some tools, however, are new and increasingly important in an online environment.

The ALMOND Virtual Communication Strategy™ is a bucket of tools based on the study of neuroscience and communication to make the virtual interaction more valuable, enhance our ability to deliver our messages more clearly and more effectively, and make it easier for the audience to remain engaged.

The tools in this communication strategy can be used in a variety of situations. This book talks about *meetings, interactions, presentations,* and *conversations,* and about *audiences, listeners,* and *participants.* Determine the context that is most relevant to your situation and apply each tool accordingly.

Each chapter that follows focuses on one letter of the

ALMOND

Audience

Now more than ever, we must be able to not only connect on a human level but to confidently switch to business even in a seemingly unnatural mediated environment. Today's listeners have short attention spans and are selfish, so it is our job as communicators to make sure we provide immediate value. Not all forms of mediated communication are equal. So once we come up with a strategy to communicate, we must also choose the appropriate medium.

Length

Being on a video call requires more focus than face-to-face interaction, and we have to work harder to process nonverbal cues like facial expression, tone, pitch, and body language. Additionally, we are on camera and are aware we are being watched. All this adds up to fatigue and is exhausting.
We need to consider how much today's audience can take in, and how quickly we can get our message across and achieve our goal.

Mirror

Of course content is important, but the experience of the meeting is equally important. To enhance our virtual presence, we need to consider "emotional contagion," which relies on the mirror neurons of the brain. We can choose what we bring to our meetings — but be aware that whatever you bring is contagious.

Organize

Today's listeners demand that we start with value and end with action. Listeners still tend to think of meetings (whether live or virtual) as an interruption of their work. Most people dread meetings and are relieved when they are over so that they can be productive again. Because of that, we need to establish value along the way and have a plan and structure in place to show that the interaction is intentional and that we are connecting to do work, not to interrupt it.

Need to engage

We don't just crave content, we crave connection. But interaction is not the same as engagement. Here are tools to not only help us make better connections to our audience, but to be better listeners and to ask better questions so we can lengthen and deepen the conversation.

Do's and Don'ts

If you were to search for articles on best practices for video meetings, you would get more than 600 million results in just over half a second, not to mention the thousands of webinars and courses. The tips and tricks and best practices can seem overwhelming, so I have created a practical curated list of do's (and some don'ts) from hundreds of articles and webinars, and years of experience, and then actively vetted the list with the help of over 3,000 professionals. This is your one-stop shop for virtual interaction tactics and how they can enhance your strategy.

Chapter One: Audience

How should you start planning a virtual sales engagement, meeting, training workshop, or any virtual interaction? Think about your audience. It is always about them; it is never about you.

What changes do we need to make to accommodate the virtual audience? Why are they attending your virtual session? What value will they get from it?

Carefully choose your medium or channel to meet today's expectations. A meeting should be a chance to connect to and with people, not just an interruption of their work. At a live meeting, we have a chance to chat individually or as a group and gain social interaction, team building, empathy, and awareness of our collective situation. In a virtual environment, however, that richness is gone. Of course, you should let everyone chat while people are joining, but make no mistake – virtual cannot be the same social experience as live. However, we can still get work done.

To start the process — and as basic as it may sound — first decide whether you have something of value or a unique experience to share that requires interaction. If you are just providing information, in today's noise-filled overcrowded message landscape, it is probably a better idea to skip the information dump during a meeting and share the information via non-synchronous channels such as documents, newsletters, text, podcast, email, or even good old-fashioned mail.

If you do need to interact in addition to providing information, try not to automatically jump to a virtual face-to-face environment. Phone calls still work surprisingly well and mitigate some of the fatigue-inducing elements of face-to-face calls.

Still think the meeting should be face-to-face? Make sure everyone is needed on the call at the same time. If there is no need for everyone to interact or if this is just a one-way communication, the meeting could be a message sent asynchronously. Don't pull people away from their jobs to join you for a meeting when they do not need to be there. I often hear the pushback on this recommendation: that even if people do not need to participate, they should be there to hear what went on in the meeting. In that case, you can record the meeting or the message and deliver it so they can look at it when it is more relevant to them.

Think of it this way: If someone had to miss the meeting, would they be able to get everything they need by watching the recording? If the answer is yes, they did not need to be there live in the first place. If the answer is no because they missed out on an opportunity to have their voice heard or to ask a question, then they should have attended the live meeting.

My grandmother used to say, "If all you have is a hammer, everything looks like a nail."

Not every meeting needs to be a virtual meeting, and now that we understand why we are so fatigued when we attend virtual meetings, we should use the tools and resources at our disposal to think more strategically. Carefully choose your channel (phone, text, document, email, etc.) to meet today's new expectations.

This simple decision tree can help you decide the best way to engage your audience.

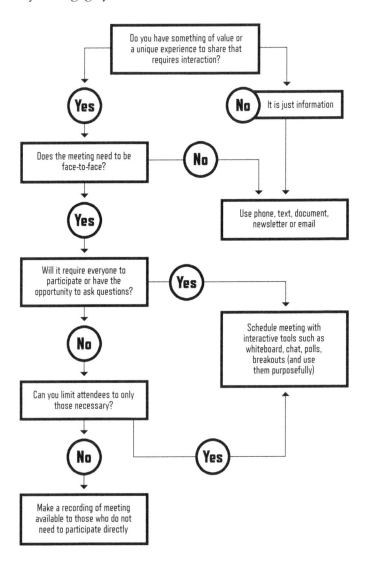

Once you decide on format, how do you start your communication? You need to get their attention. You need to lead with value.

There's a part of the brain called the Reticular Activating System (RAS), and its job is to work as a filter for all incoming information from all five senses. It helps you determine whether what is coming in is noise or whether it is relevant. There's nothing in between. If it's irrelevant, it's noise, and we move on to what's next. Remember, particularly in a virtual environment, you as the presenter are competing with emails, text messages, the family dog, children, etc. All of these distractions are telling the RAS that they are the most important piece of information at this moment.

I'm not sure if this happens to you, but very often when I am driving home, I get to my house, put up the garage door, and realize I have no idea how I got there. I was so busy thinking about what I'd make for dinner or reflecting on my day that I wasn't focused on driving. You can, of course, do two things at the same time (driving and thinking), but you can really only focus on one. The RAS makes sure of that. However, the RAS does re-evaluate relevance constantly. If an ambulance pulled in front of me as I was driving, the RAS would know that this is more relevant than thinking about dinner and would make me focus on driving once again.

The RAS keeps us from getting overwhelmed by helping us determine what to focus on, because, again, we can only focus on one thing at a time. Multi-tasking is a myth! Now, I am sure plenty of you think that multi-tasking cannot be a myth because you're good at it. If you believe you are a good multi-tasker, what you are actually good at is switching rapidly between tasks. Which sounds great, but a summary of research reported by Bryan College shows that switching rapidly between tasks lowers your IQ by 15 points and if done on a regular basis can lower emotional intelligence and lead to less brain density in the areas controlling cognitive and emotional control.[8] The American Psychological Association reports that multitasking makes you 40% less effective.[9] Multi-tasking just does not work! The RAS makes us focus on only one thing at a time. Neuroscientists call this inattentional blindness or selective attention.

As early as 1975, research on inattentional blindness garnered great attention in the scientific community. In the original study, Neisser and Becklen[10] superimposed videos of two separate activities —a hand-slapping game and people passing a basketball —and asked the study participants to count either the hand slaps or basketball passes. Then, they introduced an unexpected event (like shaking hands in the middle of the hand-slapping game). The participants did not notice the unique change in behavior if they were not watching for it. Simons and Chabris conducted a similar experiment in 1999[11] that became so well known, a TV commercial was based on it. In this study, participants watched a video of two teams (dressed in either white or black shirts) running around and passing a basketball. The researchers found that if the participants focused on counting the number of passes made by a team, they failed to see someone dressed in an enormous gorilla suit walk right through the middle of the game.

Many variations on those studies all come to the same conclusion: relevance is the key to attention.

I am sure we can all recall an instance when we attended a virtual meeting, did not see the value, busied ourselves with other tasks, and then were surprised when the meeting was over and we realized we hadn't had to listen or engage at all. Hopefully you can also recall a time when you attended a meeting, saw the value, were encouraged to engage, and were surprised at how much you got out of it. When hosting a meeting, you need to make your content so relevant that every participant's RAS decides to focus on you.

When we communicate, we must begin our message with relevance, which is especially hard now because we have our normal distractions in addition to the distractions of the medium itself (like looking at a dozen other people and faces and rooms at the same time), If we do not, we are just noise and cannot hope to get our message across.

How do you become more relevant to the listener? You help them see the value they get by attending. You help them see what's in it for them. Most of you are probably familiar with the acronym "WIIFM" — What's In It For Me. The "Me" here is always the audience. It should always be about them. Unfortunately, nobody really cares about us as communicators. The audience only cares about themselves and whether or not they will get something out of what you are about to say.

We have short attention spans, and we are increasingly selfish listeners. It's as if I have a remote control in my hand and if I don't like what I see, I will quickly keep searching for something that is more relevant. As communicators, we have to make each listener's RAS see our message as valuable enough to stop and listen. The only way to do this is with a strong WIIFM statement that is then reinforced throughout the virtual session.

When I am with my corporate clients, I often see an interaction fail simply because they did not focus on the listener and instead focused on what they wanted to get out of the meeting. If you start with something like, "I am here today to share with you some information that I found." I will instantly realize that this is not really about me and look for something more relevant. Sometimes we feel it is so urgent to get our message across that we don't consider whether it's something the listener needs as well.

The only way to engage the audience is by giving them something of value, something that they will get out of the session that they hear as the first thing.

They have to be motivated to engage.

We must have a good WIIFM statement right at the beginning of the message (after the niceties, of course) that will make the listener want more. If you don't establish relevance to the listener immediately, they simply will not listen to the rest of your message. Don't think of what you want to accomplish with the message. What will your audience get from listening to you? You must set up the session as a win-win — a win for you and a win for the audience. Be transparent and concrete about what they will get out of the information you are about to tell them, and they will be more likely to engage. A better WIIFM would be, "I have found information that will help us significantly reduce our frustration searching for documents that are misfiled." With this sentence, the audience knows what the value of the information will be at the beginning.

During the early part of the COVID-19 pandemic, I signed up for a webinar hoping to hear a tip or trick on how to better conduct a session I had done live many times but had not yet done in the virtual environment. It was free, and honestly, I figured it was probably a waste of my time. I had attended many free webinars on how to do virtual delivery better and had always been disappointed. I joined this particular webinar with the full intention of keeping my microphone on mute and my camera off, and taking a peek now and then to see if a topic was worth listening to.

I had been able to get away with that behavior before, because most of those webinars were just a method to showcase a vendor's expertise or to enhance the vendor's credibility or resume. Since it was never about me anyway, I never felt bad about not engaging. Perhaps you have been on similar calls.

In this webinar, on this particular morning, however, everything changed. As usual, I signed in, put my microphone on mute, turned my camera off, and got busy with other tasks while everyone joined the meeting. But this time, the facilitator for the session began by telling us exactly what we were going to get out of it. I loved that, because then I could decide if I should engage or completely disengage. Turns out that the content was relevant for me, so I began to listen. Soon she asked a thought-provoking question and then put us into very small breakout rooms to work out our ideas on a specific topic. The assignment for the breakout room, and the flow and timing, were simple and clear. I found that I was not able to sit on the sidelines. Because I expected to find value in what was about to happen, I had to turn on my camera and microphone and actually engage and participate. For the first time in this virtual world, I felt that I was being held accountable for what was going on and was given a voice and a reason to contribute.

Now, what I learned that day may have been covered in some of the other webinars that I had ignored. But the point is that this time, I wanted to stay and contribute. Because I was engaged, I got much more out of that opportunity than I had in the past.

That is when the power of a strong WIIFM coupled with the right environment really hit home. There is a better way to have virtual engagements. It all starts with relevance and continues with a sense of intention to carry that value through.

Chapter Two: Length

We know that it is harder and more exhausting to engage virtually. Additionally, many of us feel that we are constantly in virtual meetings.

Actually, it is more than just a feeling. In December 2019, the online meeting/video conference platform Zoom had around 10 million users. In March 2020, at the start of the COVID-19 pandemic in the United States, that number had jumped to 200 million daily users. Just one month later, in April 2020, there were 300 million daily users.[12] And that is just one virtual meeting platform.

It is easy to get overwhelmed by the amount of information we are consuming and expected to process and make sense of, so we can turn it into action. Information is no longer scarce; there is always more available. Knowledge is no longer a competitive advantage. So, in today's information overload society, once you know what you need to know, what are you going to do with it? The competitive advantage now is sound judgment and a thoughtful point of view gained not just from information, but from experience as well.

As Hal Varian, Google's chief economist and emeritus professor of information science, business and economics at the University of California at Berkeley, aptly predicted in 2009, "I do think those skills—of being able to access, understand and communicate the insights… are going to be extremely important."[13]

If connecting the dots to provide insight is the value, how much information do we really need? Since we are a society of poor listeners, it is the speaker's responsibility to help the listener understand information easily. The speaker needs to make information digestible in easy-to-chew bites and framed in a way to demonstrate value so that we can internalize it, remember it, and move toward action.

This really is all about having a clear idea of what is important to your audience and what you want to communicate. The WIIFM will set up the value, and then you must carefully pick and choose how you will use data to support the WIIFM. In today's jargon, this process is called curation. In the same way that you don't share every picture you take on your phone, you don't just provide information, you curate it first. According to an article in the *New York Times,* when listeners believe something is curated, it reassures them that what has been put together is somehow more meaningful.[14]

And that's what we all want. As a listener, I expect that before you meet with me, you will have gone through all the relevant data and evidence and distilled it down to what is most meaningful and valuable to me and my situation. This makes it specific, personalized, and meaningful.

The idea that sharing less is actually better seems counterintuitive. In the past, we considered those who could talk for a very long time and had a great breadth of knowledge to be smarter. This was part of how we established credibility. For today's short attention span audience, those days are gone. We have neither the time nor the interest to listen to it all, interpret what it means for us, and then figure out its value.

Back in the day, I knew a lot of phone numbers. Now I hardly know any. Why? I don't need to; I can just look them up. I can look up anything when I need it. So, when we talk about the importance of paying attention to the length of an interaction, we mean not just time but quantity as well. Of course, we want information, but if you can curate the information, quickly get to your point, and connect the dots for me so I can clearly see the value, that is what will drive me toward action.

While most of my clients accept that they need to spend more time preparing so that their interactions can be shorter, they often worry that if they curate their information too restrictively, they may focus on the wrong thing and lose the ability to make an impact.

You may think that your listener would like to choose from a wide variety of topics and would be more engaged if you offer them that choice. But studies have shown that more choice is not better.

A study done in 2000 by scientists at Columbia University and Stanford University observed the behavior of 754 shoppers at a grocery store that was known for its large selection of items. For example, it offers 250 kinds of mustard and 75 different types of olive oil. In the experiment, the researchers set up two different displays of "exotic" jams. Common jam flavors were removed from the study so that regular habits of selection would not influence the results.

One display of jam had 6 choices (limited choice) and the other display had 24 jam choices (extensive choice).

As you might guess, initially the wider variety of choice attracted more shoppers (60% for extensive choice and just 40% for limited choice). The interesting finding, however, was that even when more flavors were offered, the shoppers still only chose to taste the same number of flavors. And, perhaps more importantly, 30% of the shoppers faced with limited choice subsequently purchased a jar of jam, compared with only 3% of those faced with extensive choice. The researchers found that "even when choices are self-generated, overly extensive choices may have demotivating consequences."[15]

This study wasn't about communication, but the point is the same. Help the listener by doing the necessary research and curating the ideas, data, and messages that you intend to share. Of course, you need to have breadth of knowledge so you can pivot and refine what is most important to the listener as they ask questions. You want to be prepared to talk about a lot. But you must be willing to focus on delivering only one point at a time so that the listener is not overwhelmed. For any key point you are trying to make, consider that your audience is on a strict need-to-know basis.

Remember that they can always ask for more, and if they are finding the interaction valuable, they will.

Even though you have now curated your content and focused your message, in a virtual environment, how long should the initial meeting be? You of course, can sustain the length of a meeting by providing value, but I am often asked how much time you should allow when you schedule a virtual meeting. The answer seemed to have changed a bit from when we were in a live non-mediated, face to face environment.

In July 2020, approximately four months after the COVID-19 pandemic caused massive shutdowns in America, Microsoft wanted to analyze data on their newly remote workforce.

They had known that meetings had continued to gradually get longer over time and had read the research[16] showing that this trend was having a negative effect on employee productivity and happiness. With the shift to working remotely, they found that meeting duration evolved organically (not because of a management mandate) to 30 minutes or less. When they then sent out a sentiment survey, to gauge how employees felt about this new norm, this change was not only appreciated, but meetings that were scheduled for longer than 30 minutes came under more scrutiny as to why a meeting had to be that long and whether the meeting would just be a waste of everyone's time.[17]

Schedule meetings for less than 30 minutes, or be prepared to show how the increase in time will increase value. Planning the length of our interactions needs to be strategic now more than ever.

Chapter Three: Mirror

"Ideas, sentiments, emotions, and beliefs possess in crowds a contagious power as intense as that of microbes."
—Gustave Le Bon (1896)[18]

What you display during a virtual meeting or presentation is mirrored or mimicked by the audience. You can control the tone and environment during a virtual meeting by putting out there what you hope to get back. This process is called emotional contagion, and it can have a real effect on how you are perceived during meetings.

We all have a choice to decide what to bring to our virtual meetings. You can lead through motivation or fear. You can be angry or accepting.

But be aware that whatever you bring is contagious.

We are wired to mimic what we see. This mimicry serves a social function. Humans rely on connectedness and affiliation, and we have a strong need to belong. We know that mimicry is pervasive and occurs automatically. According to a textbook on social psychology, "The way a person thinks, self-regulates, feels and behaves in a given moment in time is influenced by the presence or absence of mimicry in preceding social interactions."[19]

Through modern neuroscience, we better understand how this contagion works. Every brain has a mirror neuron system (MNS). When we watch someone experience something — being hurt, or laughing, or yawning — a subset of our neurons responds as if we are experiencing the same thing.

Here's just one example. In 2016, Candace Payne donned a toy Star Wars Chewbacca mask in her car and recorded her reaction. When she opened her mouth, the mask allowed her to make the unique sound that Chewbacca is known for. The cool factor of the toy, however, was not what made her video famous. It was her laugh. She laughed so hard that the video became funny to us, too; it made us laugh and feel good. She titled her Facebook post "It's the simple joys in life," and within five days, the four-minute video had over 140 million views and became the most viewed Facebook Live video of that time. It was "reshared" on Facebook over three million times. Payne earned the nickname "Chewbacca Mom" and ended up on morning news programs and late-night talk shows, and even wrote a book about it. She received gifts of more than $420,000.[20] Why all the fuss? Her laugh and joy made us laugh and feel joy.

Another example, very common, is the contagious nature of yawning. Just seeing the word "yawn" makes many people want to yawn. (Did you just yawn?) Studies show that the responsive yawn is triggered involuntarily when we see another person yawn. Interestingly, this also happens in chimpanzees and dogs![21] This mimicking ability correlates with empathetic skills in healthy humans and is reduced in people who suffer from disorders that affect their ability to socially interact, such as schizophrenia and autism.[22]

We know that emotions are contagious, so how do we use that knowledge to enhance our virtual presence? First, use your voice and second, have confidence.

Researchers have found that the emotion listeners perceive in the voice of the presenter actually creates the same mood in those listeners. In one study, participants listened to a recording of someone telling a neutral story with either a slightly happy or a slightly sad voice. Those who heard the story told in a slightly happy voice reported being in a better mood than those who heard the slightly sad voice. In a follow-up study, participants who repeated back the content of the speech they heard mimicked the tone of the speaker. This suggested that participants adopted a mood that was the same as the mood implied by the speaker's voice.[23]

Of course, you have to be authentic, but if you start your virtual meeting or presentation sounding sad, angry, disgusted, or uninterested, your listeners will begin to feel the same way. You don't have to be happy, but you should always try to at least sound pleased to be there and to have something to share. Studies have also shown that when we hear a voice that we categorize as positive, we tend to like that person more.[24] A simple technique is to greet and welcome the meeting participants as they join the meeting. It is an easy way to communicate your desire to be there and that you are ready to collaborate.

Second, be confident. That's easy to say, but what do you do if you don't feel confident? You fake it until you make it, which is more than just folksy advice. It has been scientifically proven. Behavior can change attitude, and attitude can change behavior. If your attitude is positive, your behavior will follow, but equally, if your behavior is positive, your attitude will follow. So, if you find it hard to change your attitude, start by changing your behavior.

Let me give you two concrete examples that you can implement immediately.

The first one is simply to smile. Even if you're not feeling great, put a fake smile on your face. I can guarantee that within a few minutes, you'll already be feeling better. At least 138 different studies have proven it. In short, when our brain feels happy, we smile; when we smile, our brain feels happier. The muscles we use to smile send messages to the brain to release dopamine, endorphins, and serotonin. Even a forced smile has this effect. So turn your camera on and smile! Be intentional. It is hard to lead with our camera off and our microphone on mute!

But what about the audience? Science has identified part of the reason for a great smile's allure. In a study using functional magnetic resonance imaging (fMRI), scientists found that when participants viewed faces in focus that wore a smile, the activity in the orbitofrontal cortex — a region of the brain involved in processing sensory rewards — was stronger than when the face was not smiling. In this case, dopamine was released and caused the observer to be happier too.[25] Dopamine is an extremely potent neurotransmitter, one that is more addictive than some drugs. The release of dopamine is your brain rewarding you when you are with people who are smiling, even if you don't realize it.

We have also found that the opposite is true. The experience of pain activates the same areas of the brain for the observer of a person in pain. Those who are empathetic can even judge the pain's intensity.[26]

The second way to change your attitude by changing your behavior is to have good posture.

At least 55 studies have confirmed the reflexive link of posture. Studies show that posture affects subjects' specific emotions, affect, mood recovery, retrieval and recall of positive versus negative memories, and self-evaluations.[27]

In order to act confident, address your posture. A stooped posture can activate a negative mood and even slow down your recovery from an existing negative mood. You can use posture as a relatively efficient and robust way of regulating your mood.

Don't slouch or slump. Slouching impairs mental cognition. Raise your spine. Hold your head high and open your shoulders wide. Straighten up — but don't stiffen. Keep breathing calmly. You'll feel a boost in energy and self-confidence.[28]

Posture can not only improve your mood, it also influences how people will perceive you, your attitude, and your level of confidence. How you hold your body – often called body language – can tell more about you than your words can. Sitting up straight or standing straight when speaking are more powerful positions than slouching or stooping. Good posture indicates that you are confident, have self-respect, and respect your audience. Straight posture also says that you are interested in what the other person is saying and that you value the conversation. Slouching indicates a lack of interest in the other person and their words, or that you don't care what they think about you. Poor posture can also indicate a lack of self-esteem.

A few years back, when my book *Getting a Squirrel to Focus* became a national best-seller, I had to do some radio interviews. I prepped well for the interviews and knew my key points by heart. But since I was doing the interviews from my home office, in my first interview, I dressed casually, stayed seated – and you could really hear that in the recording, which sounded flat. For the second interview, I stood up, got dressed for a business meeting, and started it with a smile. The difference was amazing. I made the same key points and told the same stories, but you could hear the confidence.

I challenge you to try this experiment. For your next virtual presentation or meeting with your supervisor, stay seated. For the second meeting, adjust your camera, stand up tall and smile. What did you identify as the difference between these virtual engagements?

But now, what about the audience? In a series of studies focusing on the mimicry of mannerisms, researchers found a "chameleon effect": participants changed their own mannerisms to blend in with those in their current environment. Participants reported no awareness of either the presenters' mannerisms or their own mimicry of those mannerisms, providing additional evidence that this behavioral mimicry can be an automatic and nonconscious process.[29] If you start with good posture, your participants will benefit too, and ultimately everyone will be happier and more energetic for your meeting.

So, if you want to not only look more confident, but feel more confident too, fake it until you make it. We mimic to increase liking, empathy, and rapport. It brings people together emotionally. It also brings together people psychologically — their attitudes converge.[30]

How are you managing the experience of the meeting, not just the content?

You set your meeting's tone. **Be authentic** – we can now see into your living room or office or kitchen, so you are exposed. Think about your environment for a virtual meeting, reduce distractions, and set the stage for a positive and engaging session. **Be human**. If you do not seem interested in what you are saying, no one else will be either. Stand up, take a deep breath, and smile! Be authentic in your style, but bring energy to the session. This is a time for leadership, so don't begin by apologizing about the way the session will go or talk about how much you hate virtual meetings.

Be positive, be interested, be intentional, be valuable. If you bring that attitude to the session, it will become contagious.

Chapter Four: Organize

Today's listeners demand that we start with value and end with action.

We all still tend to think of meetings as an interruption of work. As discussed in the "Audience" chapter, it is imperative that you start with value, and once that is established, you must have a plan to help your listener feel engaged with curated information (but not overwhelmed) and to believe that the journey you'll take them on is intentional and valuable. Now that we realize that information alone is not as valuable as is once was, we must realize that we are always persuading, so we must always lead toward action.

Judgment and decision making are greatly influenced by the way information is positioned.

The order of the presentation affects a listener's cognitive process.[31]

We need to rethink the structure of our conversation or presentation so that the listener will give us a chance to get our point across.

Whenever I give keynotes or workshops, this is the one tool that the participants consistently rate as the most important, the easiest to apply, and the one that generates the most impact. As described below, applying a **persuasive structure** for virtual meetings, rather than a **narrative structure,** is key to establishing relevance and is even more important than when we are in a face-to-face meeting.

When preparing your virtual presentation, you can either put your key message at the end (narrative structure), or you can put it first (persuasive structure). These two triangles can serve as visual examples.

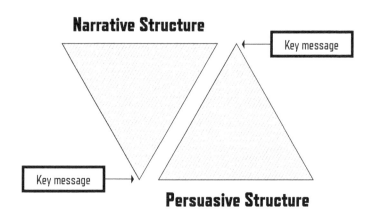

In the narrative structure, you provide the argument and detail, and then conclude with the key message. This narrative structure is how we have been sharing information for centuries. It's the way we tell stories. It's the way we pass information from generation to generation. We feel comfortable with this approach because it is so familiar to us.

The narrative approach still works at the pub or at the coffee shop. It still works around my Thanksgiving dinner table. Thanksgiving is my favorite holiday. I have an uncle named Dom, and when it's Thanksgiving, I make sure I sit near Uncle Dom and that we have some wine at our end of the table, because he tells the best stories about countries he's never even been to. And then at the end he'll say something like, "And that's because it was my shoe." I love that. It's great and it's entertaining. I could listen to his stories all day long. I don't care where the story takes me, and I don't mind a surprise ending — I may even welcome it.

But the narrative approach doesn't work in business, particularly in a virtual meeting environment.

We simply do not have the time or patience to hear you weave your tale and then finally get to your key point. We're not here for entertainment; we're here for value. With today's virtual listeners, you have to get to the point, make it relevant, and do it in the persuasive order. Therefore, in the rest of your professional career, you may never again say, "Last, and most importantly…" If it's the most important thing you have to say, it should be first. You have very little time to grab our attention and make your point before we stop listening.

When using the persuasive structure, start with a declarative WIIFM that gets the attention of the RAS (see chapter 1). Then provide the most important piece of data first, followed by the rest of your details. When the message has a high degree of relevance, putting the most important or key message first has the greatest impact on the listener. This not only makes intuitive sense, but it has also been proven to be effective by many studies.[32]

Consider a personal example from a few years ago, I was driving home after a long day of work when my husband called and asked me what we were doing for dinner. I had no idea, so I suggested that he pick up our daughter at swim practice while I went to the store to pick up a delicious, already cooked rotisserie chicken. I picked up the chicken and as I got close to my house, I noticed fire trucks, police cars, and ambulances surrounding it. My house had been on fire! I jumped out of the car, ran down the driveway, and came upon the fire chief. He saw the question in my eyes and began to tell me what happened.

He said, "At 5:32 your daughter decided she was too hungry to wait for you to come home with the chicken and convinced your husband to make her a grilled cheese sandwich instead. He got out the bread, buttered it, got out the cheese, put it in the pan, turned the stove on high, walked away, and got distracted. The temperature of the pan got so hot that when the cheese melted and hit it, a plume of smoke was sent up and set off your smoke alarm and fire detector. But don't worry. Everybody got out okay, and there's very little damage."

Now if we're at my Thanksgiving dinner table, that's a fine way to tell that story. When I use that story for a large audience during a keynote presentation, I often hear gasps when I say that my house was on fire. It's a very dramatic story. But, for me, at that moment in my driveway, what did I want to hear first? I wanted to know that everybody was okay and that there was little damage. I didn't care about the temperature of the pan, or what my husband cooked my daughter for dinner. At least, I didn't want to know the details yet. I would want to know the details later, so I could kill him, but I did not need to know them at the beginning. I wanted to know immediately that everybody was out and safe and that there was only a little damage. Then I would say, "Oh, thank goodness! What happened?" Now I'm ready for detail. I'm only ready for detail once my need for relevant information has been sated.

For highly relevant messages, the persuasive structure — beginning, "The fire is out, everyone is safe, and there is no real damage" — would have had a greater effect on how I heard the message. Since my need (relevance) was not fulfilled, I would have a hard time paying attention to the details and facts of the story. I first want the message to fulfill my need and show me how to interpret the facts, and then to provide detail and evidence.

It may feel a bit bold to put your key message first. I often get the pushback of "You want me to just say it? Just say the conclusion, first?" Yes, we want you to get to the good part faster. It feels really different because we are used to a more traditional storytelling path through the narrative, but the persuasive structure is what the audience craves. Even if this feels awkward to you at first, remember that this is not about you. It is about the audience, so you must do what is best for them.

Especially in this new virtual environment, we fill up really fast, consuming not only information from the virtual meeting but also from our environment, email, texts, etc., so we need the most impactful ideas and message first.

You must start the virtual session with a declarative WIIFM statement and let your audience know why they should pay attention.

This phenomenon reminds me of a study of how people selected breakfast foods from a buffet. The 124 participants were randomly assigned to go through one of two buffets. The first began with healthy foods (fruit, low-fat granola, and low-fat yogurt) and ended with unhealthy ones (cheesy eggs, potatoes, bacon, and cinnamon rolls). The second was set up in the opposite way: unhealthy foods first, then healthy foods.

In both buffets, people tended to fill their plate with the first food offered. In fact, over 75% of diners selected the first food on the buffet, and the first three foods on the buffet made up 66% of all the food they selected, regardless of the food presented. So the order of presentation had a profound impact on what participants put on their plate. Serving the healthy food first was an easy way to help people eat better.[33]

This same idea is true in communication. We will fill up our cognitive load and working memory with the first things we encounter. Since we do not want our audiences filling up before we can get to the key message and best evidence, a simple change in order to the persuasive structure can have a great impact on what the audience is able to take in.

Once you have started with value, decided on the order and direction of your conversation to consistently give value, connect the dots, and find meaning (not just data dump) of the curated information, there is one final piece to plan. The audience must be moved toward action. As we noted earlier, we must start with and sustain value and then end with action.

We know it is important for decisions to be made as a result of the meeting. How can we move from talk to action? How can we arrive at decisions on what needs to be done as a result of the meeting?

In order for the conversation, presentation, or meeting to be considered valuable, there should be action required to move forward.

What are the elements of a strong call to action, and how can we best arrive at a shared meaning?

Now that they have heard your message, and perhaps a summary of your message (if it was long or complex), the audience needs to know what to do. When you tell your listener your call to action, there are three things to remember:

First, be specific.

When you tell your listener what to do, be as specific as possible. Should they put together the plan, do they need to get approval, is more research needed? Exactly what should they do? If you close your meeting with something vague like, "I hope I have your support," you're leaving things up to interpretation. Do you want them to physically hold you up, or give you money, or cheer when they see you in the hall? Since we are not really sure what the "ask" is, we probably won't do anything. In contrast, if you said, "I hope I have your support and that as a result you will be the keynote speaker at our advocacy group meeting," they know exactly what they are supposed to do.

According to a British study, advice that is stated in the form of specific, concrete instruction rather than a series of general rules is more likely to be recalled and complied with. In that study, specific instructions led to higher compliance with medical advice than did advice given as general or vague rules. This was significant because a review of the evidence on rates of patient compliance with medical advice revealed that 40–50% of patients did not correctly comply with their doctor's instructions.[34]

To increase compliance with a request, the request must be specific so that the listener knows exactly what action should be taken. This is why, for example, the American Red Cross tells us to text $10 to Hurricane Relief. They don't ask us to donate what we can, which would be vague; they make it very specific so that we can make an immediate decision and act fast.

Second, make sure what you ask the audience to do is doable.

Don't ask for something that is too hard to do or an all-out commitment. Is there an easy way for them to do what you want or at least start to do it? If I do not feel like I can make a difference, I will not do anything at all. Most people, for example, will not donate money for breast cancer awareness, but they will give to help a friend raise a small amount to run in her mother's name to support breast cancer research. This effect is explained by the "empathy telescope," or psychophysical numbing.

Many researchers have tried to determine why, even after we become aware of a large-scale disaster or mass suffering, we would rather give to a single starving child[35] or a dog lost at sea.[36] One study asked participants to decide whether it would be better to provide enough water to save the lives of 4,500 refugees in a camp of 250,000 people or offer the same amount of water to a camp that had 11,000 people. A sizable number of participants indicated that they would prefer to save lives in the smaller camp—even though the number of lives saved would be identical in either circumstance.[37]

The same effect was found when it came to donating money. In this study, the participants were told that they had $10 million to spend and could either save 10,000 lives from a disease that killed 15,000 a year or save 20,000 lives from a disease that killed 290,000 people per year. Even though it seems counter-intuitive, overwhelmingly, the volunteers indicated they would rather spend the money to save the 10,000 lives.

They chose a larger proportion rather than a larger number. An intervention that saved a fixed number of lives seemed more valuable when fewer lives are at risk.[38]

Millions of children could use aid. But consider the case of Charlie Gard, an 8-month-old British child diagnosed with a rare disease that cannot be treated in the UK. The GoFundMe page that his parents set up to cover travel expenses netted roughly $1.758 million in 2017.[39] Our empathetic telescopes work best when they are focused on something we feel we can accomplish and where our help will do a noticeable amount of good.

Finally, make sure the action you ask for happens soon.

The call to action should be something your audience can do very soon after you ask. If there is too much time between asking and doing, they will lose their passion for the idea and forget.

A 2018 study entitled "The Mere Deadline Effect: Why More Time Might Sabotage Goal Pursuit" showed that even though we believe giving someone more time would benefit them by providing more flexibility and fewer restrictions, giving the person a shorter deadline is better. When we provide a longer deadline, people believe the goal is more difficult, more resource-intense, and potentially beyond their capability, which leads to procrastination.[40]

For a task that seems urgent to complete, a person is more likely to take quicker action because they believe it will be easier and require fewer cognitive demands (having to remember the task and what they need to do). Creating this sense of urgency and deadline for the next task in an action sequence plays an important role in whether or not the request you make is complied with.

The organization of your virtual conversation now looks like this:

- WIIFM
- Supporting Details (with most important point first)
- Call to Action

Only when our conversation or interaction has a clear focus, impactful persuasive structure, and purposeful guidance through the message, ending with a call to action, can we succeed at sharing meaning with a virtual audience.

Chapter Five: **N**eed to Engage

How do we keep listeners engaged in a virtual setting?

It's hard to facilitate a valuable conversation in a virtual environment while incorporating new technology. Not only do you need to determine the most relevant curated information, you have to organize that content so that the audience can handle it, have a goal in mind, and engage the audience in order to connect and share meaning.

Engagement in a virtual environment doesn't happen by chance. It has to be planned, much like the planning you'd do if the session were live.

Keep in mind that interaction is not the same thing as engagement. Just because you take a poll, for example, does not mean that you have engaged the audience. Remember that we crave connection. If possible, engage your audience in conversation so they feel that they were needed, had a chance to find their voice, took a moment to reflect and got something of value for their participation.

Having questions already prepared will help keep the conversation on track and strategically require the participants to think and reflect. Your job is to steer the conversation toward something that will be valuable to everyone. Having a framework in mind is the biggest key to successful facilitation.

The ORID Method: Objective questions, Reflective questions, Interpretive questions, and Decisional questions

In 1984, David Kolb synthesized three models of development (those of John Dewey, Kurt Lewin, and Jean Piaget) into a method to enhance experiential learning—that is, learning by experience.[41] Researchers who focused on understanding the process[42] refined the theory,[43] and it was further refined by R. Brian Stanfield in his book *The Art of Focused Conversation*.[44] The result is what we now consider the natural sequence and logical progression we go through when making decisions, following a natural human process for effectively focusing a conversation. The method is also called the discussion method and the basic conversation method.

The ORID Method has four stages of questions that can guide participants through the material to move a meeting or presentation forward. You should use this process and planned questions *after* opening a virtual meeting with a declarative WIIFM statement. After all, why would the audience answer questions without first seeing the value of their involvement?

The ORID process is a handy tool to gather collective wisdom and structure the flow of the meeting or conversation. The questions can be developed before the meeting start so that the facilitator has the chance to focus on the dialogue and help draw connections and conclusions. Keep in mind that these questions, and their progression, are meant to be not a script, but a guide. This is not usually a "one question per level" method, and depending on the conversation you may have to go back to a previous level before proceeding to the next level. As the conversation continues, other clarifying questions may need to accompany the ORID questions, so it is not an all-or-nothing approach.

An additional benefit of a sequence of questions is that it provides the opportunity to get back on track if the conversation or meeting has gone off on a tangent. I often see facilitators struggle to get drifting conversations back on track. Some drift may be beneficial, but if you need to get back to the conversation as planned, you can ask another ORID question from the next level.

The sequence of these levels of questions is important. We are leading our listeners through a natural-seeming decision-making process. We don't want to jump around in this process. If possible, maintain the order of the levels of questions.

Objective questions

The first level of question, the O, is the Objective questions. These questions draw out facts, explore observations already present, and provide a baseline of understanding and interpretation.

Examples of these questions may include:

- What is the history of this?
- What resources do we have?
- What are we trying to achieve?

In the O section, we are asking open-ended questions that have no single right or wrong answers. In fact, there may be multiple answers to these questions. This is an opportunity to get people thinking about the topic and make sure there is a base level of understanding among all parties so that decision making can move forward. If this is not the first time you've had this conversation or covered this specific topic, and you know that you share a base of information about this topic with them, you may want to skip this step. But this should be done rarely, as the step helps people refocus and recall what is already known.

Reflective questions

The next level of question, the R, are Reflective questions.

This set of questions helps evoke emotions and provide a relationship to the data. In business, this step is often overlooked because it seems too "soft." But the need for emotion is paramount when trying to persuade. When emotion is present, the decisions made tend to be strengthened.

Examples of these questions may include:

- How do you feel about that?

- What feels most challenging or worries you?

- Have you found the process to be frustrating?

- What most excites you?

The R encourages listeners to begin to make connections and further identify their experience with the topic. They can reflect and begin to internalize the conversation. This is the point in the conversation that usually uncovers objections to or questions about the plan or product and can illuminate bias or hesitancy with moving forward. If this step is skipped, the conversation remains much more superficial, which is not ideal if we are trying to persuade. Remember that the definition of persuasion is not to win the argument, but to move the listener toward a new belief or action. You cannot be moved toward a new belief or action if you are not moved by the argument.

Interpretive questions

Interpretive questions help participants think more critically and make sense of the situation. These questions help uncover a deeper value, meaning, significance, or implication.

Examples of these questions may include:

- What have we learned so far?
- What insights have you gained from this?
- What does this mean for us?
- How does this affect our work?
- What are some underlying issues?
- What is the importance of this?
- What options are open to us?

These questions help identify patterns and determine their meaning to the larger picture. They also give the listener an opportunity to articulate underlying insights. In this step, you want to make sure that the data, facts, and evidence that you have shared are understood and interpreted in the way you intended. By checking in with this level of understanding, we can arrive at shared meaning, not just shared facts. Only then can we hope to move together along the same path of action.

Decisional Questions

This series of questions helps pull together insights and ultimately make decisions and priorities. The participants now can decide on commitments to move forward.

Examples of these questions may include:

- What do you think we should do?
- How does this fit our priorities?
- What are the next steps?
- What does this mean for our future?

Here is an example that highlights the ORID steps in context and demonstrates how closely they mimic a natural decision-making process. Let's say I'm trying to decide whether I should buy the latest iPhone to replace my current one. My first step is to start with the "O" to determine what I know about the phone, its features and benefits, cost, specifications, etc. I need to do the research to provide a baseline of knowledge before I can move on. I ask myself questions like, "How much do you know about the phone?"

Once I have a baseline, I ask myself reflective questions about the new features to see how I feel about the prospect of getting a new phone. Am I overwhelmed with the new features? Am I excited about having a better phone? Am I frustrated with my existing phone? As I reflect, I realize that I am very frustrated with my phone and excited about having a newer model.

Since I did not uncover strong objections or relate to negative reflections, I'm ready to make a decision. I then interpret what I learned. In this case, I realized that the features and benefits of the new phone would undoubtedly solve my frustrations with my old phone. I would be able to take better pictures, finish tasks more quickly, and not run out of battery so fast. The insight I gained from this process convinced me that investing in a new phone is a good choice for me. Lastly, once my decision is made, I need to take action and plan the next steps to fulfill my decision.

In other words, ORID translates into What, So What, Then What, and Now What—the logical path I would take to decide.

Of course, for more complex issues, the R questions might uncover objections (like price or concern about saving my data), and I might have to do more research and go back to the O, or I might decide that the new model does not fix my issue and the insight I gained confirmed that I should not get a phone.

This is not a sales model or a manipulation tactic. This method helps the conversation move along a logical flow to a conclusion without going off on a tangent. Following this process is more intentional and shows we have a plan to help our listeners make a decision.

Key to this strategy is using open-ended questions. Open-ended questions that require specific examples and illustrations work best. Specific questions that can be answered with yes or no may limit discussion. Remember to let people think. Try to guide the listeners through the entire process to get to your end goal. As you work your way through the session, constantly move from the known to the unknown. Even if everyone begins to agree, answer questions with other questions to probe or move to the next area of interest. Try to prompt participants with a variety of questions that require different levels of thinking.

Summarize vs. Synthesize

The ORID process has to take place as a conversation, so active listening must also be involved. When we take part in a conversation, we are more likely to listen first in order to respond, and *then* in order to understand. Take your time and process the information. To get from one level to the next, work on not just summarizing what was said, but synthesizing what was said. There is a big difference. For example, read one of Aesop's most famous fables (and where the term "sour grapes" came from).

The Fox & the Grapes

A fox one day spied a beautiful bunch of ripe grapes hanging from a vine trained along the branches of a tree. The grapes seemed ready to burst with juice, and the fox's mouth watered as he gazed longingly at them.

The bunch hung from a high branch, and the fox had to jump for it. The first time he jumped he missed it by a long way. So, he walked off a short distance and took a running leap at it, only to fall short once more. Again, and again he tried, but in vain.

Now he sat down and looked at the grapes in disgust.

"What a fool I am," he said. "Here I am wearing myself out to get a bunch of sour grapes that are not worth gaping for."

And off he walked very, very scornfully.

Now, think about how you would summarize the facts of the story.

You might say that there was a fox who saw some grapes that he wanted. They were high so he had to jump for them. He tried a few times but failed and then left.

I could ask a dozen people to summarize the key points of that story, and the results would be close to identical. The summary does recapture what happened, but it doesn't give us the richness of the meaning of the story.

Now, think about how you would synthesize the meaning of the fable so that you can gain insight from it. What moral would the story have? What is it trying to teach us?

You might believe that the fox should not have given up so fast, or that he should have chosen a more attainable goal so that he would not have become so frustrated. You might think that the fox needed to think outside the box to get what he wanted, or that just because he couldn't get the grapes, that didn't mean they weren't good.

We can think of many lessons from this fable and can interpret the facts in many ways. In doing so, we can then have a richer, longer, and deeper conversation that explores nuances instead of just agreeing or disagreeing on facts.

So, after each level of ORID, don't be in a hurry to jump to the next level. Don't just summarize what people have said and move on. In workshops or breakouts at national meetings, I often see the facilitation of sessions fail precisely because of this missed opportunity. The facilitator finally gets everyone involved in a good conversation and is getting input from the participants. A participant may add an insightful piece of information, but because the facilitator is not listening for an opportunity to delve deeper, they simply say, "Thank you for that. Who's next?" or "That was a good question. Does anyone else have a question?" If the input was insightful or a good question, pause and engage in the conversation.

Listening is an integral part of the communication process. If we go in with the mindset to be insight-oriented, not just fact-oriented, we can increase the quality and value of the conversation.

This type of intentional movement through the ORID process will help the participants either as a group or a 1:1 virtual meeting become more fully engaged, move the audience to action, build your credibility and also help establish your leadership style.

Chapter Six: Do's and Don'ts

Now that you have your strategy, you are ready for tactics.

Once businesses started to shift to more virtual interactions, there were hundreds if not thousands of articles, webinars, e-learnings, and job aids online to help you run a successful virtual meeting or presentation. While this book has been mostly focused on the strategy for better virtual communication, we cannot afford to overlook the tactics.

In early drafts of this book, more than a few readers told me that my introduction was too generous in assuming that most people already know that the camera has to be near eye-level, so people don't look up our noses; or that people realize that backgrounds can be distracting, and we would rather look around your very interesting office than listen to your message; or that everyone should start the meeting on mute; or that if you are in front of a window or bright light, you will look like you are in a witness protection program.

Initially, I disagreed with them, since I had seen many professional-looking webinars early in the shift to virtual. Upon reflection, however, I decided they were right. As I joined more and more virtual conversations, I began to notice a disregard for the tactics of virtual conversations, which resulted in far less than ideal sessions.

Perhaps we are trying to regain some of the relaxed, casual conversation we used to have in person. Perhaps we are uncomfortable with feeling vulnerable and showing our colleagues the inside of our houses. Maybe we're just unsure how to make it better.

I think we are all craving connection and want to build relationships the way we did when we were physically together. Early in the COVID-19 pandemic in the United States, I was on a business call and we were chatting a little before we started our business conversation. One participant who arrived a bit late told me within about three seconds that she knew I was cool and felt she would like me because of my background. I thought that she meant my academic background and accomplishments, but before I could even say thank you, she told me how much she liked the style of my room. I have some old exposed brick in my office, and she thought that was cool, so she thought I was cool. I was flattered, but thrown. If we were in person, I would have more quickly determined she was looking around the room and then commented, and that would have been a natural rapport builder. In this environment, that simple, relaxed comment seemed out of place and reminded me how different the virtual environment is.

Unless you already had a perfectly appointed office that reflects your personal style, many people struggle to find just the right place in their home to use for these calls. Most of the time I see hooks on what is now a newly bare wall to try to keep the background clean. If you are comfortable with it, though, you can let your personality come through in your background, as long as it is not distracting. In one of my workshops, a participant insisted on using one of those fake digital backgrounds, because otherwise she felt her privacy was being invaded. A digital background might feel better for you as the presenter, but it is not ideal for the audience. After all, we know you are not in outer space or on a lovely beach somewhere. The backgrounds were fun at first, but they don't work very well if you move around, and they can be distracting. A bare wall is better than a fake background. (A professional green screen might be an exception here).

And then some people are trying so hard to make a better environment, but are not sure how to manage it. One meeting participant was focused on trying to reduce background noise created by her young kids. So she did her presentation in the one place where she could find peace: the bathroom. Because of a bad camera angle, we could easily see that she was sitting on her toilet. When I asked her about it, she said it was the only room in the house that was quiet because the kids knew not to disturb her when she was in there.

With a simple switch of the camera, the back of her toilet was hidden, and her frame did not give away any secrets.

Whatever the reason, we have to realize that virtual communication is here to stay. Once the COVID-19 pandemic subsides, our use of virtual platforms may diminish, but I believe they will still be part of the fabric of how work gets done for a very long time. Because of this, we have to marry good strategy and good tactics if we hope to be successful in this new way of communicating.

The following list came from dozens or articles and webinars and years of experience, and has been vetted by over 3,000 professionals! I hope it helps your sessions improve, not just for you, but for all of us who sit through them. Please notice that the preparation list is longer than the presentation list.

▼ When You Prepare

Do:

☐ Have strong and predictable internet service

☐ Provide hand-outs electronically as a pre-read or as a supplement if content is heavy

☐ Plan to present from a quiet place

☐ Have someone in charge of tech if possible so the presenter can focus on presenting

☐ Consider your background; be sure it is clean or not distracting – we often want to see more of your desktop or the office and not listen

☐ Plan to have your face fill most of the screen, since that is what will convey energy and mood

☐ Test your platform ahead of time and make sure you know how to work it properly

☐ Have a contingency plan if things go wrong. If there is a critical error, end the meeting and reschedule to another time or different medium.

☐ Have slides that are more visual than you'd use for a live presentation, especially if we do not see you and only see your slides. If you stay on one slide too long, we may think it is a technical error

☐ Have a plan for when to take questions

☐ Do a dry run in advance

☐ Have some water nearby

☐ Go to the bathroom before you start

☐ Open the session five minutes early so you can casually chat with participants and they can chat with each other. Have your video on as soon as the session opens. It is more welcoming.

☐ Be willing to give up control sometimes. It is not all about you. Just be sure you have a plan to regain control to move the meeting along if necessary.

☐ Be aware that this might be viewed on a mobile device and make it easy for that audience too.

☐ Put a brightly colored Post-it note or a pair of googly eyes next to the camera. It will occasionally draw your eyes up and make us think you are looking at us.

☐ Dress appropriately – it changes your sense of professionalism, and you might have to stand up, or might plan to stand.

☐ Turn off electronic notifications, so there is no disruption of your attention.

Don't:

☐ Use a fake digital background if possible

☐ Be lit from behind. Adjust lighting so you are front lit. Being back lit makes you look like you are in a witness protection program

☐ Have your camera below your face. Make sure the camera is at or slightly above eye level (we do not want to look up your nose)

☐ Open with "good morning." If you are presenting globally or across time zones, use a more general opening.

▼ While you present

Do:

☐ Manage your time

☐ Use your face and voice strategically to enhance content

☐ Feel free to call people by name. If possible, let them know that they will be asked to share or comment

☐ Allow for peer interaction as well as just presenter-to-participant interaction

☐ Let participants know if you are going to be silent to give them a chance to think

☐ Stand while you deliver if possible – it changes the energy, breathing, confidence, etc.

☐ Have good posture

☐ Maintain eye contact with the audience (look at the camera instead of yourself). It gets easier to do with practice.

☐ Establish ground rules (everyone on mute, raise hand to talk, cameras on, etc.)

☐ Be civil and respectful

Don't:

☐ Don't *ever* intentionally embarrass anyone.

☐ Don't go off on a tangent; we won't go with you. Know where you are going, so you stay on track

☐ Don't just summarize the meeting, make sure you synthesize the insights

☐ Don't start late or end late (end on time, or a little early)

Conclusion and Final Thoughts

Keep in mind that the ALMOND Virtual Communication Strategy™ is a toolbox. It is not an all or nothing approach. It provides strategies to make virtual communication, either in a group setting or a one-to-one interaction, more valuable to those who attend.

To that end, start by choosing one or two of the tools we explored in the ALMOND and apply them to your next meeting. The more tools, the better.

You now understand the importance of having a strategic communication path and have an effective new way to plan each virtual session and make your messages more persuasive, concise, and impactful—and have your audience move to action.

It is critical, perhaps now more than ever, that we embrace a growth mindset. A growth mindset is not just an open mind. If you have a growth mindset, you believe your talents can be developed through hard work, failures, good strategies. and input from others.[45] The only way to be successful in an ever-changing environment is to continue to upskill and be ready for whatever challenges are next. If we can continue to keep slowly evolving, we can prevent the need for a complete revolution of our skills and knowledge down the line.

When put into perspective, the communication change we are currently in the midst of is not revolutionary. How our audiences are changing and our need to constantly adapt to find new ways to connect, provide meaning, and interact—these have been shifting for decades. Our virtual world is the next evolutionary step in communicating and connecting. We will get back to a balanced state where we can once again connect in person instead of predominantly virtually, but I believe we will never again go back to the way things were before the virtual world was created.

John Maxwell, an expert in leadership and author of several *New York Times* bestselling books, said some years ago, "Change is inevitable, but growth is optional."[46] That depicts perfectly our current crossroads. Most people I have spoken to don't like the "new normal." Change is hard, and it is easier to ignore it or decry it or feel angry or frustrated or saddened by it. But it is also inevitable. We can get stuck here and draw the hard line on how we prefer to communicate and connect and share ideas, or we can once again evolve and grow.

This will be a great opportunity for growth.

Notes

1. Margaret Grayson. "Burlington Resident's Zoom Meeting Meme Goes Viral." *Seven Days*, 18 Aug. 2020, www. sevendaysvt.com/LiveCulture/archives/2020/04/07/burlington-.

2. RW3 Culture Wizard. *2018 Trends in High-Performing Global Virtual Teams.* content.ebulletins.com/hubfs/C1/Culture%20Wizard/LL-2018%20Trends%20in%20Global%20VTs%20Draft%2012%20and%20a%20half.pdf.

3. Manyu Jiang. "The Reason Zoom Calls Drain Your Energy." *BBC Worklife*, BBC, 22 Apr. 2020, www.bbc.com/worklife/article/20200421-why-zoom-video-chats-are-so-exhausting.

4. Katrin Schoenenberg et al. "Why Are You So Slow? – Misattribution of Transmission Delay to Attributes of the Conversation Partner at the Far-End." *International Journal of Human-Computer Studies*, vol. 72, no. 5, 2014, pp. 477–487, doi:10.1016/j.ijhcs.2014.02.004.

5. Nicola Binetti et al. "Pupil Dilation as an Index of Preferred Mutual Gaze Duration." *Royal Society Open Science*, vol. 3, no. 7, 2016, p. 160086, doi:10.1098/rsos.160086.

6. Liz Fosslien and Mollie West Duffy. "How to Combat Zoom Fatigue." *Harvard Business Review*, 14 Aug. 2020, hbr.org/2020/04/how-to-combat-zoom-fatigue.

7. Patricia W. Linville. "Self-Complexity and Affective Extremity: Don't Put All of Your Eggs in One Cognitive Basket." *Social Cognition*, vol. 3, no. 1, 1985, pp. 94–120, doi:10.1521/soco.1985.3.1.94.

8. "Millennials Multitasking in the Workplace." *Bryan College*, 6 Feb. 2018, www.bryan.edu/multitasking-at-work/.

9. "Multitasking: Switching Costs." *American Psychological Association*, 2006, www.apa.org/research/action/multitask.

10. Ulric Neisser and Robert Becklen. "Selective Looking: Attending to Visually Specified Events." *Cognitive Psychology*, vol. 7, no. 4, 1975, pp. 480–494, doi:10.1016/0010-0285(75)90019-5.

11. Daniel J. Simons and Christopher F. Chabris. "Gorillas in Our Midst: Sustained Inattentional Blindness for Dynamic Events." *Perception*, vol. 28, no. 9, 1999, pp. 1059–1074, doi:10.1068/p281059.

12. Mansoor Iqbal. "Zoom Revenue and Usage Statistics (2020)." Business of Apps, 20 July 2020, www.businessofapps. com/data/zoom-statistics/.

13. "Hal Varian on How the Web Challenges Managers." *McKinsey & Company*, 13 Feb. 2019, www.mckinsey.com/ industries/technology-media-and-telecommunications/ our-insights/hal-varian-on-how-the-web-challenges-managers.

14. Lou Stoppard. "Everyone's a Curator Now." *The New York Times*, 3 Mar. 2020, www.nytimes.com/2020/03/03/style/ curate-buzzword.html.

15. Sheena S. Iyengar and Mark R. Lepper. "When Choice Is Demotivating: Can One Desire Too Much of a Good Thing?" *Journal of Personality and Social Psychology*, vol. 79, no. 6, 2000, pp. 995–1006, doi:10.1037/0022-3514.79.6.995.

16. Constance Noonan Hadley and Eunice Fun. "Stop the Meeting Madness." *Harvard Business Review*, July-August 2017, hbr.org/2017/07/stop-the-meeting-madness.

17. Natalie Singer-Velush et al. "Microsoft Analyzed Data on Its Newly Remote Workforce." *Harvard Business Review*, 30 July 2020, hbr.org/2020/07/microsoft-analyzed-data-on-its-newly-remote-workforce.

18. Gustave Le Bon. *The Crowd: A Study of the Popular Mind*. E. Benn, 1896, p. 127.

19. Tanya L. Chartrand and Rick Van Baaren. "Chapter 5: Human Mimicry." *Advances in Experimental Social Psychology*, 2009, pp. 219–274, doi:10.1016/s0065-2601(08)00405-x.

20. "Chewbacca Mask Lady." *Wikipedia*, Wikimedia Foundation, 2 Sept. 2020, en.wikipedia.org/w/index.php?title=Chewbacca_Mask_Lady.

21. Beverley J. Brown et al. "A Neural Basis for Contagious Yawning." *Current Biology*, vol. 27, no. 17, 2017, doi:10.1016/j.cub.2017.07.062.

22. Sharat Gupta and Shallu Mittal. "Yawning and Its Physiological Significance." *International Journal of Applied and Basic Medical Research*, vol. 3, no. 1, 2013, p. 11, doi:10.4103/2229-516x.112230.

23. Roland Neumann and Fritz Strack. "'Mood Contagion': The Automatic Transfer of Mood between Persons." *Journal of Personality and Social Psychology*, vol. 79, no. 2, 2000, pp. 211–223, doi:10.1037/0022-3514.79.2.211.

24. Vanessa Van Edwards. "Vanessa Van Edwards, Lead Investigator at Science of People." *Science of People*, 19 July 2020, www.scienceofpeople.com/about/.

25. Eric Jaffe. "The Psychological Study of Smiling." *Association for Psychological Science — APS*, 11 Feb. 2011, www.psychologicalscience.org/observer/the-psychological-study-of-smiling.

26. M. V. Saarela et al. "The Compassionate Brain: Humans Detect Intensity of Pain from Another's Face." *Cerebral Cortex*, vol. 17, no. 1, 2006, pp. 230–237, doi:10.1093/cercor/bhj141.

27. Amy J. C. Cuddy et al. "P-Curving a More Comprehensive Body of Research on Postural Feedback Reveals Clear Evidential Value for Power-Posing Effects: Reply to Simmons and Simonsohn (2017)." *Psychological Science*, vol. 29, no. 4, 2018, pp. 656–666, doi:10.1177/0956797617746749.

28. Lotte Veenstra et al. "Embodied Mood Regulation: The Impact of Body Posture on Mood Recovery, Negative Thoughts, and Mood-Congruent Recall." *Cognition and Emotion*, vol. 31, no. 7, 2016, pp. 1361–1376, doi:10.1080/02699931.2016.1225003.

29. Tanya L. Chartrand and John A. Bargh. "The Chameleon Effect: The Perception–Behavior Link and Social Interaction." *Journal of Personality and Social Psychology*, vol. 76, no. 6, 1999, pp. 893–910, doi:10.1037/0022-3514.76.6.893.

30. Tanya L. Chartrand and Rick Van Baaren. "Chapter 5: Human Mimicry." *Advances in Experimental Social Psychology*, 2009, pp. 240–241, doi:10.1016/s0065-2601(08)00405-x.

31. Richard Buda and Yong Zhang. "Consumer Product Evaluation: The Interactive Effect of Message Framing, Presentation Order, and Source Credibility." *Journal of Product & Brand Management*, vol. 9, no. 4, 2000, pp. 229–242, doi:10.1108/10610420010344022.

32. Curtis P. Haugtvedt and Duane T. Wegener. "Message Order Effects in Persuasion: An Attitude Strength Perspective." *Journal of Consumer Research*, vol. 21, no. 1, 1994, p. 205, doi:10.1086/209393.

33. Brian Wansink and Andrew S. Hanks. "Slim by Design: Serving Healthy Foods First in Buffet Lines Improves Overall Meal Selection." *PLoS ONE*, vol. 8, no. 10, 2013, doi:10.1371/journal.pone.0077055.

34. Peter W. Bradshaw et al. "Recall of Medical Advice: Comprehensibility and Specificity." *British Journal of Social and Clinical Psychology*, vol. 14, no. 1, 1975, pp. 55–62, doi:10.1111/j.2044-8260.1975.tb00149.x.

35. Daniel Västfjäll, et al. "Compassion Fade: Affect and Charity Are Greatest for a Single Child in Need." *PLoS ONE*, vol. 9, no. 6, 2014, doi:10.1371/journal.pone.0100115.

36. Shankar Vedantam. "Beyond Comprehension: We Know That Genocide and Famine Are Greater Tragedies than a Lost Dog. At Least, We Think We Do." *The Washington Post*, 17 Jan. 2010, www.washingtonpost.com/wp-dyn/content/article/2010/01/11/AR2010011102007.html?sid=ST2010011304181.

37. Paul Slovic et al. "Informing Decisions to Prevent Genocide." *SAIS Review of International Affairs*, vol. 32, no. 1, 2012, pp. 33–47, doi:10.1353/sais.2012.0007.

38. David Fetherstonhaugh et al. "Insensitivity to the Value of Human Life: A Study of Psychophysical Numbing." *Journal of Risk and Uncertainty*, 1997, pp. 283–300.

39. Melina Glusac. "The Most Successful GoFundMe Campaigns of All Time." *Insider*, 16 Nov. 2018, www.insider.com/best-gofundme-campaigns-2018-11.

40. Meng Zhu et al. "The Mere Deadline Effect: Why More Time Might Sabotage Goal Pursuit." *Journal of Consumer Research*, vol. 45, no. 5, 2018, pp. 1068–1084, doi:10.1093/jcr/ucy030.

41. David A. Kolb. *Experiential Learning: Experience as the Source of Learning and Development*, 2nd ed. Pearson Education, 2015.

42. R. Brian Stanfield (ed.). The Art of Focused Conversation: 100 Ways to Access Group Wisdom in the Workplace. New Society Publishers, 2005, p. 24.

43. Laura Spencer. *Winning through Participation: Meeting the Challenge of Corporate Change with the Technology of Participation*. Kendall/Hunt, 1998.

44. R. Brian Stanfield (ed.). *The Art of Focused Conversation 100 Ways to Access Group Wisdom in the Workplace*. New Society Publishers, 2013.

45. Carol Dweck. "What Having a 'Growth Mindset' Actually Means." *Harvard Business Review*, 13 Jan. 2016, hbr. org/2016/01/what-having-a-growth-mindset-actually-means.

46. John C. Maxwell. *I Do Know This about Growth. Change Is...*, 2013, www.facebook.com/JohnCMaxwell/photos/i-do-know-this-about-growth-change-is-inevitable-growth-is-optional-to-grow-you-/10151620381877954/.

Acknowledgments

I don't really think of myself as an author, even though this is the third book I have written. I like to think of myself as an interpreter. The academic literature in the studies of communication, psychology and neuroscience is full of rigorously researched theories of how we communicate and understand communication and how our behavior affects the outcome of those processes. There are science backed keys on how to understand and make better the way we communicate in the virtual world, yet most people neither have access to nor prefer to read academic papers. Because of this, I enjoy pulling tips and gems from the literature and creating toolboxes of ideas that are immediately applicable to today's communication environment.

I use the word "interpret" here with two different meanings. I interpret the language of the academic literature and translate it into a less scientifically driven vernacular, and I interpret the studies to draw out the meaning of them as one would interpret or draw out the meaning of a play or piece of art. Of course, interpretation is always somewhat subjective and to see if one interprets the work in a way that is useful in real-world scenarios, a great deal of help is needed.

I would first like to thank my generous friends, colleagues and family members who not only gave their time but jumped into this toolbox with a leap of faith and helped me refine early versions of the work to make it more resonant. Ann Railton and Dee Walker provided great clarity of thought and gave so freely of their time and expertise with no hesitation when I asked if I could run some new ideas by them. Their input and vision of how to make the work more impactful was incredibly helpful.

And then there was Jill Benko. Jill and I were commiserating on the painful virtual experiences that we had both been enduring and she asked if I had any ideas about how to make it better. I gave her a quick outline of some thoughts and asked her what she thought. Even though she was amazingly busy, within a day, she not only read what I wrote, but had a crystal clear vision for how it could fit into the training she was doing for her company and worked tirelessly to refine these academic musings into a solid foundation for those wanting to do better in the virtual environment. Her generosity of time, expertise, spirit and passion were essential conversations to bring this book to completion.

At the onset of the COVID-19 pandemic, so much advice was being offered about how to do a better job in the virtual environment that I hesitated to add anything because I thought it might just be redundant. Then I realized that what was really needed was a better strategy and not just more tactics. A turning point for me in this realization was watching Bridget Mullins facilitate a session. She is truly one of the most gifted facilitators I have ever watched. She knows how to bring her warm and authentic style to the session to create a fantastic environment. She also always has a plan, and her sessions seem purposeful and valuable. When I signed up for her webinar, I fully intended to have my camera off, keep quiet and just listen in to see if I could pick up a tip or two. Before I knew it (and not sure how she made me) I had my camera on and was fully engaged and participating. The richness I got from that experience and not just the content motivated me to learn more and dig deeper into what we must do to not let our listeners go through yet another mind-numbing webinar with no connection.

Lastly, I would like to thank those that help turn my ideas into something more tangible. Janice Fisher is not only the best, but also the kindest editor I have ever met. David Laughlin once again worked his magic with my layout and design and thankfully keeps saying "yes" when I again want to put a squirrel on the cover of my book.

GETTING A SQUIRREL TO FOCUS IN THE VIRTUAL WORLD

NOT JUST CONTENT, BUT CONNECTION

CPSIA information can be obtained
at www.ICGtesting.com
Printed in the USA
BVHW080021250721
612595BV00002B/90

9 780986 124815